VOICES

by

BMESTL

Vol.1

Copyright © 2020

Educational Conduits LLC

The words that follow have been crafted by Black male educators who dedicate their careers to helping other educators, their communities, but most importantly, their students.

While we acknowledge there isn't one unilateral Black male experience in education, there are some common threads that many of us have endured and can discuss.

Through the triumphs and tribulations, one thing is for sure; Black males have an innate passion and skill set to serve students. Furthermore, we are desperately needed in the field of education.

To our younger brothers who are beginning to consider career options, regardless of your experiences in school or what someone may have told you about your future, please give careful consideration to the field of education.

To our brothers who are currently in education, thank you. Please proceed onward. Your value could never be quantified, and your impact extends well beyond anything you could imagine.

To all others, we ask that you read the enclosed personal stories and understand that many of the most effective Black men in education were never encouraged to pursue a career in education. Imagine what we could do if we shifted the narrative.

-**BMESTL** (@bmestl)

Forward

As a long-time advocate for improving the educational outcomes of African American children, I was very encouraged when I learned about Black Men in Education St. Louis. In focusing on not only increasing the number of black males in education but also on creating a system of relationship building, networking, experience and insight sharing, Black Males in education has great potential for making schooling more productive for black students by giving them role models to emulate and broadening their perspectives about possibilities in their lives. During my fifty-plus year work life, I had the opportunity to learn from older brothers and to motivate and inspire many young guys.

My career was very diverse and included the military, business, government, education, and non-profits. I worked with and for white men, black men, black women, and white women. The existence of racism was always there, but I decided that I had to find ways to deal with it. My mother taught me that I was not inferior to anyone based on the color of my skin. That lesson always was a motivator for me. I shared that with the many young black people that I interacted within all the areas in which I worked. BME embraces this tenant.

When I retired some years ago, there was an editorial page article in the Post-Dispatch about me and my career. It was entitled, "Can't be about you." It quotes me as giving the following advice to younger people interested in pursuing careers in public service. "Read all the time so that you understand and know what the challenges are and determine how and when you want to make a difference. Don't be swayed by loud voices and naysayers. Be willing to take risks in doing things differently. We know what doesn't work. Be able to work with people and build teams. It can't be about you. You are a cog in the wheel, but there is a wheel." I think these ideas will help BME be successful in attaining its mission and vision.

Finally, I know that working collaboratively with other organizations is crucial for BME. Indeed, school superintendents, teachers and teacher organizations, DESE, colleges of education, and youth-focused not-for-profits must be included in this vital project. The media must also be included in messaging that "Black Male Educators Matter."

-**Ronald L. Jackson**

Table of Contents

1. Introduction
2. Finding My Voice Through Others
3. Leading While Black In The 21st Century
4. An African American Male as An Object Lesson in Predominantly White Spaces
5. Defying Plateaus in Racial Equity for High-Quality Reading Instruction
6. Purpose
7. Grit Is In Our DNA
8. Overtly Fixed Racism In School Leadership
9. Protecting Black Bodies In St. Louis
10. My Journey
11. Mental Armor
12. Outro

Introduction

If you consistently have something worth saying, but you don't feel comfortable or confident sharing it due to a fear of how it will be received, you are in a state of persistent despondency.

For many students and educators who look like me, this feeling has been normalized, resulting in us exercising our right to remain silent, even in spaces where our voices are desperately needed.

Consequently, members from different identity groups feel the need to speak up for us. While appreciated, it's also important to understand that advocacy without empowerment simply leads to a cycle of palatable oppression, a mental space where I previously resided.

My coping mechanism? Writing. Which was, by far, the most effective form of processing the many thoughts I had. Even the ones that questioned if I was "educator material."

In 2015, some of my thoughts resulted in me writing a short film titled, *Speak,* a story of a young Black teenager who was given the task of writing a 2-minute speech on any topic of interest.

As the world around him awaited the grand jury results of Darren Wilson, the officer who shot and killed Michael Brown Jr. in August of 2014, this young Black teenager struggled to find the exact words to express his feelings. Not because he didn't have much worth saying, but because he was so accustomed to people speaking for him. Simply stated, making decisions for Black men, without listening to Black men, has become a societal norm.

But once he spoke the truth, what was shared was undeniably powerful and liberating.

Five years later, I can't help but wonder how many Black male educators are living as the main character in their own iteration of, *Speak*, stuck between despair, identity, and purpose.

What's more, television screens closely resemble the same unrest that we've seen time and time again. Add the emergence of a global pandemic were wearing masks as a safety measure has become the norm, Black males have been wearing a different type of mask as a way to cope with a different kind of virus that's in the air.

Unfortunately, survival for so many Black males in education rests on ventilators that promote silence as a vaccine that is as dangerous as hydroxychloroquine.

But there is a silver lining. When a group of people stands together to support each other through pain and struggles, the result leads to authenticity, purpose, and a collective voice.

As co-founder of BMESTL, nothing is more rewarding than helping my Brothers overcome the challenges they face in the field of education. For the ten Black male educators, you are about to learn from; these challenges now serve as part of their unique story. And our stories allow us to be relatable for our students.

I ask that you embrace the vulnerabilities, perspectives, and courage required to speak the truth.

To Brothers Joseph, Jim, Michael, Julius, Luke, VaShawn, Keith, Neil, Bryan, and William, thank you for this undeniably powerful and liberating experience.

I present to you, *Voices, Volume 1*

-**Dr. Howard E. Fields III** (@hefields3)

Finding My Voice Through Others

It was the first day of school for a beginning music teacher. He had just taught for the first time professionally, coming out of college and ready to make a difference. Everything was going to plan that day. The kids were excited to meet their new leader in music. They loved the musical gifts and talents of his singing throughout the day. The atmosphere was set for music to be taught.

His last class of the day, a kindergarten class, in fact, just walked in. He instructed the five-year-old future budding musicians to sit on the carpet, led them through some songs, and mimicked some funny dances. They chant the music rules on how to be respectful, responsible, and safe in his classroom. Then he asked if anyone had any questions. One of the kids raised his hand and asked, *why was he so brown?* The first-year music teacher wasn't expecting that kind of problem on the first day and quickly answered that *'God made him this way.'*

I would like to say that the story above is a true story, and it happened to this music teacher writing this essay. At the time, the answer I'd given to the five-year-old boy with brown hair and blue eyes was true. God did make me to be *'so brown,'* and I was not ashamed of it. However, when I look back, I always catch myself laughing. It has always been so intriguing that a five-year-old would ask me a question about my skin color. It was with such innocence and naive that I couldn't get mad at him. In his eyes, he didn't know why I was a different skin color than him. I don't even think he has never seen anyone outside his own color before.

Fast forward now, six years later. My first kindergarten class has graduated from being elementary school children to young men and women in sixth-grade students. It's amazing to see how much they have grown up right before my eyes. It also is amazing that I, their music teacher, has played a major part in their development. Think about it; I've been educating the next generation for 72 months, 313 weeks, 2190 days.

Was it easy for an African American young man to teach the next generation of students in a rural school district, a world that was different for him? No, it wasn't. However, every second of it has been the most rewarding experience in my lifetime. My kids have made such a huge impact on me, teaching me their cultures of farm life, four-wheelers, and country music. Not only have they taught me, but I know I've taught them as well. My students left my classroom, knowing about proper singing, rhythm counting, and how to make four-measure phrases. I also had the opportunity to introduce my kids to some of my cultures of hairstyles, different types of food, cultural books, and music filled with the sounds of Motown, gospel, jazz, and a bit of hip-hop (clean of course). Our school has become some sort of a melting pot filled with many ideas, concepts, and ideologies.

Someone recently told me in one of my graduate study classes that my presence will make a huge difference in my students' lives. He said that being exposed to someone that is different than them, and they respect will change their perceptions throughout their lifetime. Surprisingly, I am now grasping what he is talking about. Sure, it may have taken me six years to realize it, but I have been blessed with the special assignment that I know I was handpicked to do. I am more than just a music teacher to some kids. To them, they see me as a leader, a problem solver, a grown-up, a human, and yes, even a hero to some. I'm like Superman they can depend on; a Batman that can come just in the nick of time. I'm like the Black Panther that fights for the betterment of each and every child, every day.

We all know that we are living in some of the darkest times in our modern-day history. We are still in a pandemic with the COVID-19 that robbed our students their school year. You turn on the television and see the racial injustice and unrest from the people rising. Some people may say that history and time are just repeating itself like always. That may be true, but this time it's different. This time we cannot escape it. The eyes and ears are everywhere with social media and video. Everything that was done in the dark is now coming into the light. The question that we, as educators, must ask isn't necessarily what are we going to do about it? I believe the question that has to be answered is are we prepared for the challenge. In August, we are going to see our kids again. Most of them are going to have opinions heard from their loved ones, their own thoughts and questions they need to have answered. Again, are we up for the challenge?

    I believe that one of the ways we can deal with racism and problems with race relations is to have the conversation. I know it's not much, but teaching our kids that everyone is different creates a sense of empathy, something that is really missing in our country right now. Our kids need to know that the world out there is bigger than their own backyard. I had to learn that growing up. I had to understand that God created us and love us all. There's not one race or group of people that he loves more. He loves us all the same because we are all the same. The blood inside our veins is the same color. We shouldn't be fighting one another. Instead, we should be doing what we teach our kids to do, and that is to build one another up with love. That's what the world needs right now, love and understanding of each other.

Sometimes, I wish we could live in a child's world again. I can recall the days when I was an elementary school kid. I had both black and white friends. I knew that they were different from me but, as a child, I didn't see that. I saw what Dr. King said for us to see, the content of the character. I can only hope that the children that I was blessed to educate will look at another person and not judge them by the color of their skin, but judge them on their character. I have hope that they will be able to do that. I have that slim hope that this next generation will be able to do what our past generations could not, to show love towards their fellow brothers and sisters around this nation.

Joseph Moore is the Music Educator of North Elementary, Millersville Elementary, and Gordonville Elementary in the Jackson R2 School District in Southeast Missouri. His love for music started as a child, developing young voices and gospel choirs all throughout his youth. After graduating from Southeast Missouri State University with a Bachelor of Music Education, Joseph seized the opportunity to further train young musicians and share with them the same love for music that he developed. During his six years of teaching, Joseph has created North Elementary's first treble choir, simply named North Select Singers. This organization is known for giving back to the community through song and has blessed many lives through Christmas Caroling, Veteran's Programs, and Spring Tours. Just recently, North Select has been honored to sing at a National Major League Baseball game, an once in a lifetime experience for some.

Currently, Joseph Moore is working towards a Masters of Music Education at Lindenwood University. He is passionate about developing the mindset, skills, and character in future musicians that allow them to chase their dreams and passions while making their communities and world a better place.

Leading While Black in the 21st Century

Often times growing up, I would hear this notion that I would have to "work twice as hard" to reach my full potential, to be deemed equal to my white counterparts, but most importantly, be accepted by those that are in the majority. That advice has been ingrained in me and serves as my foundation in the pursuit of my career goals.

In America Needs More Black Men Leading Its Classrooms, Dani McClain (2016) states, "America's teachers are disproportionally female (75 percent) and white (83 percent), according to recent federal data. Black men make up less than 2 percent of teachers, though minorities now make up a majority of students in public schools." When I apply this same lens of data analysis to my local context, I discovered there is less than 1 percent of Black men in administration in the state of Kansas, according to the Kansas Department of Education. With that being said, serving as one of the "one percent" in my district has placed me in unchartered territory, inciting feelings of being alone, questioning my leadership style, not feeling validated in my role as well as having limited access to mentors with shared experiences. The experience of leading while Black can be overwhelming. Although some of the emotions described here come with leadership in general, in my experience, my white colleagues have not had to grapple with these emotions to the same degree as Black leaders.

Leading while Black; the title alone can be off-putting to some; because adding race makes some people uncomfortable. As I continue to grow in my career as an educator, I have the responsibility to ask questions that expand boundaries. Not just for me and my career, but for the Black male leaders who come behind me. Why are kids of color not enrolled in Honors or AP courses? What is holding them back, the teachers, or the lack of access? What professional development or training is being provided for staff around building relationships with all kids, not just the kids who come prepared? Asking questions around implementing cultural celebrations, highlighting an inequitable curriculum, and speaking up about shady discipline practices that place the kids of color at a disadvantage are examples, just to name a few. Even as I reflect and look at leaders that came before me who were men of color, there has always been a subtle questioning or second-guessing, an initial mistrust, feelings of defiance, or outright lack of respect by society. Look at President Obama, he made a lot of positive strides during his tenure as president, yet members of Congress, the media and the general public constantly undermined him, questioned his authority and looked for him to make a mistake. Trust me, if President Obama had some dirt, America would have found it. Is it sad that I feel the same way? Michelle Obama's famous quote, "When they go low we go high," sounds nice in theory, however, can be difficult. I feel sometimes, America is waiting for me to fail or fall in the traps of stereotypes that have been set by mainstream society. I'd like to think that I am optimistic and that I can defy all odds, but it's outright tiring to constantly compete in a game that one truly can never win.

Leadership is hard by itself; learning to be selfless, standing for what is right, having a vision, being mentally tough, and leading with no regrets. But leading while Black, causes one to be aware of its audience at all times, take in consideration of his/her actions in public, what is shared on social media, how they represent their identity or cultural beliefs, how they speak to staff and students; particularly of another race but most importantly how one responds to adversity and failure.

Keeping it Personal, Local, and Immediate

As I enter my seventh year in administration, the job continues to get tougher as educators are forced to reconcile the ever-changing society, technological advances, evolving testing expectations, and the recent increasing insinuation in certain spaces that educators now share the responsibility of raising their students. At age 35, this will be my fourth year as a lead principal. Being a building leader can be tough with all the demands placed on schools. Is it fair to suggest that being young and Black adds an extra layer to the equation when leading a staff? The image of a school or district leader has changed in the last ten years, which sometimes brings about assumptions that since one may not have 20 years of experience, then they might not be as effective. How does one go about building relationships as a Black leader to foster trust with its stakeholders? Often, when entering a new educational space, people ask me, "So what do you teach? Many times, at work, I have been mistaken for the coach or the security guard.

    As I reflect on where I am in my journey; leading a predominately white school, in a high achieving predominantly white school district, I can't help but think about the many nights I have reflected on my approach, my language, my attire, my vision; in an effort to be the right fit for the school. Is this what leadership feels like? Should I have to sacrifice to survive? Constantly, thinking about if I wear my dashiki's, my HBCU Apparel, or African bracelets or chain would it offend my white parents or staff. In the state of Kansas, schools are making strides to have a conversation around race and the role it plays in education. Some districts still ignore that race matters. One thing I know for certain is that at some point, students will have to interact with people who do not look like them in their lifetime. At some point, students will have a boss, a college roommate, a co-worker, an in-law that might be different than them. I hope that schools across the state take into consideration not only is it important for all kids to see teachers of color in the classroom, but they must leaders of color as well.

Healing is Essential for Endurance:

There have been times in my career where I have needed to heal from my own trauma. The stress of having to feel like I need to be perfect in my position to keep my job. This notion of working twice as hard as I have mentioned previously can be tiring and unhealthy for educators who want to be effective in this work.

In the summer of 2018, I was fortunate to attend the Beyond Diversity Institute in Chicago to sharpen my skills as a diversity leader to help lead my staff through our district's equity work. Not only did I receive great development, but I also found myself dealing with some unresolved emotions in my own equity walk. During one of the breakout sessions, I shared a moment with my group about a time when I felt the lowest in my career as a Black leader. I shared with them a picture of me that was taken from the school website and altered into a Black Face. The picture was then tweeted out on the school web site. I was a second-year assistant principal in an all-white high school. I felt humiliated. I shared with my group that I left my job in tears, second-guessing if I even belonged in the field of education.

The facilitator told me to stop and put the picture away. He was disgusted and appalled that I had endured this experience. He went on to name the fact that this was a traumatic experience. I had never really looked at it like that. I knew it was a racist act, but I felt it was my responsibility to lick my wounds, get back up, and keep fighting the good fight. The presenter shared with us that it's hard to fight the good fight when your hands are tied by trauma. I started to think how many times had I reflected on the picture and leveraged it as motivation to be better or to prove to others that I belonged, which in the grand scheme of things was a false hope in my eyes. The hope that my actions or results would change how people respected me. The bottom line is that I can work twice as hard and do well in my job but, some still may view me as less effective than my white counterparts. I can't say I have fully healed because I work crazy hours, and I feel that comes with the job, but I would be a fool not to admit to myself that I still believe the leash is short and expectations are high. I found that working harder or receiving praise and results doesn't mean that you have healed. Understanding your worth, showing up in your authentic self, and not sacrificing what you value is the start to true healing.

Why is this conversation necessary?

There are many Black leaders that feel they may not be enough, that in order to survive in certain educational settings, one has to tone it down or leave their identity at the door when being in leadership. It's crucial to have this discussion about leadership, race, and the impact they both have on our educational system. I have two black sons who I am raising to be confident, smart, and to live with integrity. My hope is that one day regardless of what system they are in, it will be fair and diverse with a curriculum that reflects many cultures and provides opportunities for them to have choices once they leave high school. Teaching my sons, the unspoken truths of being Black in America is an entirely different discussion that takes place in Black households. The conversation of bringing awareness to this topic is important because often people of color need a space for mentorship, a sense of validation, and a support group to encourage, sharpen and empower authentic leadership.

Dr. Keith Jones (@drjonrs) will be entering his 15th year in education. Dr. Jones has held leadership roles at the middle and high school levels since 2012. Dr. Jones has served as a middle school principal in Lawrence Kansas for the past five years leading Billy Mills Middle School. He currently has a new role at Platte County High School as the head principal. He has taught English, Journalism, and Video Production in the classroom. Dr. Jones is a graduate of Florida A&M University, Pittsburg State University, and Baker University, where he holds a bachelor's degree in Journalism, a master's degree in Instructional Leadership and a doctorate degree in Educational Leadership Dr. Jones is passionate about teaching the whole child and helping students develop life skills, and brings experience working in corporate America and community organizations, as well as advocating for college and career preparatory programs. Dr. Jones has two sons: Leonjay (19) attends Mid-America of Nazarene University playing football and Keith Jr. (8), and who will be attending third grade. He is a member of Phi Beta Sigma Fraternity, Inc., The BLOC (Brothers Liberating Our Community), and serves on the AMPLIFY Committee that empowers educators of color.

An African American Male as An Object Lesson in Predominantly White Spaces

Life in America as an educated, and some will say, as an accomplished African American male, is tenuous and tricky. For better or for worse, I often find myself in predominantly white educational spaces. This all started at the University of Kansas in Lawrence, Kansas, as an undergraduate engineering student. I was frequently the only African American male in my engineering classes. As a former associate professor of Christian Ministry Studies at Lindenwood University, I was often the only person of color in the classroom. Quite frankly, I do not know if being in these predominantly white spaces is a blessing or a curse. One thing is for sure when in these predominantly white spaces, I serve as *an object lesson* for my white brothers and sisters.

I attended the Sundance Film Festival in 2020: *my favorite classroom*. After landing in Salt Lake City, I proceeded to the Enterprise Rental Car service desk. I must admit, when my host first asked me to rent a car, I was somewhat bothered. Space does not allow me to elaborate here. In the end, I enjoyed the benefits of having a rental car.

Soon, I was on my way to Park City, UT. Up I went because Park City is at a higher elevation. The mountains were beautiful and majestic in Salt Lake City and Park City; especially, those draped in snow. The highway was curvy, and maybe that was on purpose. Finally, I arrived at a home in Park City, UT, that was graciously donated to *us* to lodge for the week. I entered the code to lift the garage door. I entered an empty home (my housemates were attending a swanky event tonight sponsored by my host). For five days, I lodged with several others—13 others to be exact—in this huge house (a house with seven bedrooms, three floors, a laundry room on every floor, and countless bathrooms).

I explored the home with some trepidation. Why? Because I am thinking to myself, "I am an African American male in this predominantly white space." Instinctively, I interrogated myself, "Am I on a hidden camera being watched by, who I presumed to be, white homeowners? Will I soon hear police sirens?"

All the bedrooms were taken, it appeared. So, I waited for my room assignment. Eventually, my housemates began to arrive. I met Stan. Stan was once upon a time a member of a trio that did impromptu comedy like what we see on Saturday Night Live. Paige (Stan's wife) arrived and informed me where I would be laying my head that week: a spacious bedroom with its own bathroom. Paradise! However, I was a bit uneasy too; because adjacent to my room was a bunkbed furnished room with several white females. Did I mention I was the only African American male in this humongous home? It was hard to relax; it was hard to breathe because it seems I must shoulder all the burden to be on my absolute best behavior. In the words of Michelle Obama, "When they go low, we go high." I had to make a concerted effort to remain *high* because there are no second chances. My deportment must dispel misconceptions about Black men. I am an object lesson for my white brothers and sisters. Our nation's Black-White history makes what seems to be normal—sleeping next to a room of white females—abnormal and precarious. Of course, this made me think of a previous field trip with college students.

Field Trip

During my time at Lindenwood University, MO, in St. Charles, MO, a catastrophic EF5-rated multiple-vortex tornado devastated a large swath of Joplin, MO. Recovery and rebuilding would take years to complete. My colleagues, 'Susan' (Social Work Professor), 'Shannon' (Philosophy Professor), and I organized a trip to Joplin for an educational, hands-on, field trip. Several students signed up to go. I drove one 12-passenger van with Susan, my co-pilot, in the passenger seat; Shannon drove the other 12-passenger van.

Again, I was the only African American male professor among all whites and mostly females, at that. This event is funny now, but when it happened, I was terrified. Showers for men and women were in a trailer outside our dorms. I got up early as I normally do and headed to the shower. I repeated as I walked to the trailer, "Men showers on the right side; women showers on the left side." While I was showering and enjoying some solitude, I suddenly heard a female voice, "Where is the shampoo?" I froze. I whispered, "Did I enter the wrong side of the trailer? O crap!" Immediately, I started thinking about the worst-case news story on the front page of the local newspaper: "DR. LUKE BRAD BOBO, AN AFRICAN AMERICAN MALE AND ASSOCIATE PROFESSOR IN CHRISTIAN MINISTRY STUDIES, ENTERED THE FEMALE SECTION OF THE TRAILER SEEKING TO ASSAULT A WHITE FEMALE STUDENT WHILE SHE WAS TAKING A SHOWER."

There are a plethora of cases in history where a white female's account was regarded as factual, and the Black male stood no chance: *guilty until proven innocent*. I instantly thought about the creatively titled book, "Picking Cotton: Our Memoir of Injustice and Redemption." Ron Cotton, an African American male, was picked out of a line up for raping a white female; the only things—he did not do it; he had a solid alibi. Nevertheless, he was sent to prison for ten years for a crime he did not commit. At last, DNA evidence exonerated him of these false charges. Recently, I read, "At the Dark End of the Street: Black Women, Rape, and Resistance--A New History of the Civil Rights Movement from Rosa Parks to the Rise of Black Power," by Danielle McGuire. This book repeatedly illustrated that the Black male was not given the benefit of the doubt and often convicted unfairly by all-white juries.

Back to Joplin, the first trip

Still wet, and quietly as I could, I grabbed my toiletries and jolted out of the shower, passing the shower stall occupied by this white sister. I was later exonerated because I learned from Susan that this mysterious white female admitted to her that she had entered the male section of the trailer by mistake. Whew, maybe I would have been given the benefit of the doubt?

Because of this field trip, these books, our nation's dark racial history, the testimonies of ancestors and family members, and the daily experiences of Black men like me, I was anxious because my room was adjacent to a room of several bunk beds, occupied by all young white females. I found it hard to relax because I had to work overtime, not say or do something that might be perceived as out of place.

Dreams Deferred, Dreams Unfilled

I viewed the Sundance film, *Miss Juneteenth*. What an educational film! Many Americans and African Americans are likely unfamiliar with Juneteenth. Juneteeth is "an American holiday that commemorates the June 19, 1865, announcement of the abolition of slavery in Texas, and more generally the emancipation of enslaved African Americans throughout the former Confederate States of America, outside Native American lands" (*Wikipedia*). Many young African American women who previously participated in this *Miss Juneteenth* pageant went on to do noble things; some became judges and lawyers; others became politicians.

Not so for Turquoise, who won this pageant as a teenager. Turquoise was a waitress in a seedy bar and restaurant in the hood. Vicariously living through her daughter, who was born out of wedlock, she gently coerces her to enter the pageant. Slightly rebellious, the daughter does not win the pageant. The ending of this film was somewhat predictable because I have seen such 'scenes' play out in my own family.

After seeing *Miss Juneteenth*, I boarded a city bus to the Latter-Day Saints Church. As I rode the bus, I thought more about *Miss Juneteeth,* and I thought of Langston Hughes' poem, "A Dream Deferred." Turquoise had to settle for a life of deferred dreams. Many African Americans have had their dreams deferred or permanently canceled. These lines from Hughes' poem seem to fit Turquoise's situation (and the situation of many African Americans):

What happens to a dream deferred?
Does it dry up
Like a raisin in the sun?

Or fester like a sore--

And then run?

    I am Turquoise in *Miss Juneteeth* because I have had dreams deferred; one dream that seems to be out of my reach in America is experiencing racial diversity, equity, and equality. Dr. Martin Luther King, Jr., the dreamer, dreamed:

I have a dream that one day this nation will rise up and live out the true meaning of its creed: "We hold these truths to be self-evident; that all men are created equal."

I have a dream that my four little children will one day live in a nation where they will not be judged by the color of their skin but by the content of their character.

    While much of King's dream has been fulfilled, much more remains to be fulfilled. Because of this gap between the fulfilled and unfulfilled, because I am not considered equal by many, and because it appears my white brothers and sisters' eyesight is impaired by lack of knowing the Black history and the Black experience, I must be vigilant to be a person of character, especially in predominantly white contexts, because I might not be given the benefit of the doubt due to the color of my beautiful skin.

Home Sweet Home

I saw many other moving and provocative Sundance films during my stay in Park City, UT. Alas, I had to leave my favorite classroom. And I was glad to be going home; I was no longer an object lesson. However, I was wondering, "What did my white brothers and sisters learn?" Home sweet home provides me a refuge; home sweet home allows me to let my guard down and speak Ebonics if I desire. Finally, I could breathe. I could relax. I did not have to be on my absolute best behavior. Home sweet home affords me a moment to reflect on what I learned and what I hope others have learned. Will this narrative—being an object lesson, a minority in a predominately white space—replay again? Yes, it will. I am certain of that.

Luke Bobo (🐦@lukebbobo1) serves as director of strategic partnerships for Made to Flourish (Overland Park, KS) and brings a rich blend of experience to this organization, having worked for 15 years in the marketplace as an engineer before pursuing a Master of Divinity and Ph.D., and eventually serving as the executive director of the Francis Schaeffer Institute at Covenant Seminary. Luke also holds a Bachelor of Science and Master of Science degrees in Electrical Engineering.

Luke spent time as a professor of Christian Ministry studies at Lindenwood University (St. Charles, MO) and wrote curriculum for a workplace ministry. Luke is a visiting instructor at Covenant Seminary, Cru's Institute for Biblical Studies (IBS), and Meachum School of Haymanot.

He is also the author of *Living Salty and Light-Filled Lives in the Workplace*, *A Layperson's Guide to Biblical Interpretation: A Means to Know the Personal God*, and

Race, Economics, and Apologetics: Is There a Connection? He has co-authored two books: *Discipleship with Monday in Mind* and *Worked Up: Navigating Calling After College.* He has also written on varied topics such as human cloning, rap music, technology, race/racism, work, film, ethics, and apologetics. Luke has spoken domestically and internationally. And he has been interviewed for many podcasts and has been quoted in the *New York Times*.

He is married to Rita S. Holmes-Bobo, and they have two adult children: Briana Amber and Caleb Avery.

Defying Plateaus in Racial Equity for High-Quality Reading Instruction

As we embrace the winds of change in this viral season, it is important to help our black boys develop a sense of identity in every classroom encounter. Fearless social-emotional learning means our scholars will become more self-aware and reflective about their identity. More black male educators seek to empower students and ask the tough question that is forever at the forefront of their minds. The question for black male educators to answer who goes beyond the en vogue chats on watered-down equity conversations and implicit bias training is how I become more of an agent for change in a marginalized school that thinks systemically, but acts locally?

Equity is the new vitamin water, and every school and classroom across public education sectors of the country have their own flavor that they choose to tout. We cannot just default and use the word equity because it is fashionable. I have learned to begin with racial equity to systemically rid our schools of all inequalities. Public education in America was never charged to educate all children equally and to high standards and therefore results in inequity by design. Over the summer home, gyms were being created, and videos surfaced of people doing push-ups, sit-ups, biking, jogging, and enjoying the outdoors as COVID-19 closed spas, pools, and local health clubs. Cities started to reopen, and the fitness and healthy eating waned when the public began to go out and get out of the house. A certain plateau was reached, causing the routinized way of meal prep and home exercise to fade away. When we consider how they fade, let us consider the plateaus of racial equity in our classrooms and how we can become confederate in the way we attack the loss of momentum on the path to racial equity.

Literacy is the key to freedom for those who want racial equity. I am a black male educator, and I recount and retell the stories to many of my students of the nights our ancestors worked the cotton fields and stayed up late trying to learn the alphabet and attempting to read the bible. Too often, in our attempt to defy plateaus in racial equity for high-quality education, we forget that cultivating agency and self – identity are the starting block in the race to close gaps in literacy levels. Too frequently, black boys quickly lose all interest in any type of reading. I have talked to many that state they do not see why they have to read, and they don't see the relevance in what they are asked to read in our classrooms. Approximately a quarter of the total children's books produced in 2015 were picture books, and about half of those depicted nonhuman characters (e.g., animals, trucks, etc.). The percentage of characters from diverse backgrounds are a follows 0.9% American Indian/First Nations; 2.4% Latinx: 3.3% Asian Pacific/Asian Pacific American; 7.6% African/African American: 12.5% animals, trucks, etc.; and 73% White (see Cooperative Children's Book Center, n.d.).

In order to defy plateaus, we have to ask is it illiteracy of aliteracy. Our scholars must know the true definition of reading, and we must be convicted of the fact that they have lost interest in reading (aliteracy) because they don't see themselves in their reading. We cannot deceive our black boys and girls in espousing the ideals that they are empowered and beloved if they are not lauded and celebrated in the texts in which we place in our lesson plans and in their hands. While defying plateaus in racial equity, scholars will have to determine the central ideas or themes and summarize key supporting details to show mastery in literacy. Determining the meaning of words used in a text and clarifying the meaning of words used in a text are the literary and informational text standards for mastery and proficiency in reading. Belief and influence rest firmly in the black male educator's hands. What we believe are important influences every decision that we make about the content we nobly teach, how much fidelity we use in teaching, and who we believe should receive the content that helps students develop a positive image and become social agents for change locally.

Black history is a separate branch of African history that extends beyond its borders, but we must begin to help them at a young age see themselves through mirror and window texts that reflect their black history and perspectives.

Black stories are the American stories that have been historically omitted from the texts in our classrooms. Perhaps we could beat the odds for our minoritized students if we decolonized our approach to reading whether it be in a virtual or brick and mortar school setting. I have been reminded over the course of my twenty-plus years in education if education is lacking any relevance, it becomes utterly meaningless. If we don't engage our black boys in creating a healthy self-identity and a love for literacy, we will inevitably crash or plateau. If a text is not a mirror, why ask scholars to start at chapter one and place them in the pain of reading on the glory and exaltation of another whose experiences and story never mimic their own story. The most widely read book ever published, the Bible has never been read in absolute order, and it has kept millions engaged over time and space. The voice of racial equity in our schools says stop forcing black students to read in ways that are unnatural to them.

Several educators have made a clarion call to our leaders to stop blaming all educational inequity on poverty. Proficiency rates in literacy for whites and African Americans who are economically disadvantaged are disproportionate. If poverty was the root cause, why are poor whites showing higher reading proficiency rates than poor African Americans across the United States?

Let us not be weary in this race to lead and defy the plateaus of racial equity. High-quality instruction means representation live and in our new virtual space. Our curriculum and instructional materials have to reach to be a mirror to help our students see and be seen, historically, so they can be agents locally for change. Our texts and high-quality instruction also emerge into a window to enable them to climb out of to become successful literate learners. When we choose to democratize our classroom, scholars will choose to read about and become their authentic selves.

A child cannot be taught by anyone who despises him, and a child cannot afford to be fooled. –(James Baldwin)

Dr. Michael Lowe (🐦@m1lowe) served in public education for over 23 years in Memphis, TN. He is married with three children that range in age from 14 -2 years of age. He started teaching 5th-grade mathematics and social studies in a small classroom at Ross Elementary in the Fall of 1997 after graduating from the University of Memphis. He was promoted to assistant principal in 2001 and served at Southwind Elementary School until 2005. Michael graduated with a doctorate in Educational Leadership from Union University and was promoted to the office of principal in the summer of 2005 at Millington Middle School in the Shelby County School system. Dr. Lowe served as Executive Director of Curriculum and Instruction in 2012, and Regional Superintendent in 2013-2015. He is currently the Equity Officer of Shelby County Schools (SCS). SCS is the largest school district in Tennessee. Dr. Lowe also serves as an adjunct professor at Christian Brothers University, where I teach Supervision and Instruction. This has led him to work alongside many talented educators as a consultant with the Tennessee Department of Education (TNDOE) in the newly adopted administrator and teacher evaluator programming and facilitation.

Purpose

Written for my K-1 students at City Academy; Founding Principal (1999)

Published in "Me! Ten Poetic Affirmations" (2014)

Do you want to know what I can do?

Do you want to know, am I true?

Sit on down and let this phenomenon show you!

I am the hope from yesterday.

I am the truth now.

I am tomorrow's way.

I am Purpose! Yes!

That's right! Purpose!

That's me! I can call answers from the past.

I can cook and make it last.

I can sing and make the music swing.

When I use my mind, I can do anything!

I am Purpose!

Yes! That's right!

Purpose! That's me!

I am passionate.

I am peaceful.

I am productive. I am Purpose.

I am soulful. I am serene.

I am selective.

I am Purpose.

Do you want to know who I am?

Do you want to know what I can be?

Open your eyes, and I know you will see.

I am Purpose!

Yes!

That's right!

Purpose!

That's me!

Julius B. Anthony

(🐦@stlblackauthors) is Founder and President of St. Louis Black Authors of Children's Literature and The Believe Project. Julius has enjoyed more than 20 years as an early childhood and elementary education professional and has served as a classroom teacher, principal, director of curriculum and instruction, and adjunct professor. Throughout his career, Julius has enjoyed writing motivational poems and short stories for his students and serving as a fierce advocate of literacy-based PK-12 education. In October of 2014, Julius published his first children's book entitled "Me! Ten Poetic Affirmations," which debuted at the National Black Child Development Institute's annual conference in Detroit, Michigan.

Also, Julius B. Anthony is the Founding Principal of City Academy, a successful independent day school located in north St. Louis city. One achievement Mr. Anthony is particularly proud of is his current upstart "The Believe Project," which seeks to ensure all children are confident and competent readers by the end of third grade. Through a unique partnership with Scholastic, Nine Network St. Louis (PBS), IKEA St. Louis, Ready Readers, and We Stories, Believe offers new and innovative ways for children to have access to culturally responsive books. In its inaugural year, four Believe sites opened throughout the St. Louis metropolitan area: Ferguson Community Empowerment Center, Sister Thea Bowman Catholic School (East St. Louis, IL), Glasgow Elementary in Riverview Gardens School District; and Old North Confluence Academy. On July 3, 2020, The Believe Project premiered as a literacy-based children's show in response to the regional demands for K-3 remote learning. The show aired on Nine Network PBS Channel 9 and Missouri History Museum's "Storytime in the Museum" summer platform.

Additionally, Julius volunteers with distinction on several Boards including Riverview Gardens Education

Foundation, St. Louis Regional Literacy Association, Missouri Literacy Association, Turn the Page STL, Atlas Public Schools, United Way Early Childhood Allocations Panel, Books for Newborns, and Howard University Alumni Club of St. Louis.

Julius B. Anthony is a proud graduate of Howard University (Washington, DC) and Clark Atlanta University (Atlanta, GA). Julius is also a 2001 graduate of Leadership St. Louis and a 1995 fellow of Washington University's (St. Louis, MO) National Endowment for the Humanities' (NEH) Harlem Renaissance Project. He is a recipient of the 2017 Artist Support Award from the Regional Arts Commission of St. Louis, 2018 BALSA Foundation Summer Fellow, first recipient of the Children's Education Alliance of Missouri's IDEA Award (2019), Inner City Connections Fellow (2019), St. Louis Civic Pride Foundation's 2019 Civic Pride Champion Award, and DELUX Power 100 Award (2019).

Grit Is In Our DNA

GRIT is the ability to show resilience to be able to bounce back from an unfortunate situation. I have seen no one embody the definition of GRIT or worked to instill it in me more than the greatest woman ever to walk the planet, the one, and only Louise Smith. Who is Louise Smith, you ask, Louise Smith was my granny. She was born in 1933 in Greensboro, NC, during a time of radical change in our country. With little more than a 5th-grade education and carrying her firstborn child, my grandmother migrated to the Northwestern part of Ohio, Toledo, to be exact. My granny would go on to bear eight more kids, and from them would come over 40 grandkids, of which my granny would play an instrumental role in raising all of them. My grandmother played an instrumental role in providing grandmotherly wisdom; also, many of us had to live with my grandmother from time to time as my mom and some of her siblings all have spent time in prison. She was extremely monumental throughout my life, starting from when my mom had me at the ripe young age of 16. From the day I was born, I feel that based on the stories I've heard, it was my granny's' mission to ensure that her grandchild would not allow life setbacks to dictate where he would ultimately end up.

My granny was my number one cheerleader, and this was never more evident than in the many times I was suspended from school. I was suspended so often that I believe if you were to go back and look up my cumulative school folder, it would be a few volumes to make space for all the suspension letters I received. However, each time I was suspended and sent home, my grandmother would always ask the questions, how do we take this situation and turn it for good? What lesson could we pull from the misbehavior that took place in school today? Even when I was expelled from Robinson Jr. High my 8th-grade year and had to attend an alternative school. Through her disappointment, my granny still couched her conversation as to how I can use this opportunity to better myself. In 9th grade, somehow, it all came together and clicked for me.

Reflecting on the many discussions and learning from my mistakes coalesced and fueled me to graduate from high school. Those lessons served as fuel for high school and as the undercurrent that pushed me along through college, when I felt like I wouldn't make it, in times when professors made me feel like I didn't belong. Even when one professor asked if I was in the right class, my grandmother's encouragement pushed me to keep going towards the bigger prize of education.

    What does all this have to do with GRIT? If you read carefully, you will see that GRIT isn't built overnight or after one setback. GRIT is built over many setbacks. It took GRIT for me to reach my academic goals and achieve the success I have today. However, this GRIT isn't realized until I reflect on the road it took me to get where I am. I believe this is true for all people. When you are facing adversity or a setback, you don't think of GRIT, you think of purpose, you think of your goals, and you think of past victories that helped you overcome the moments you've faced. So please understand you can't teach GRIT from a Social Emotional Learning lesson or a talk during an advisory class once a week. GRIT is an internal driving force that has to be nurtured and cultivated.

When I think of the school I lead and my beautiful black and brown students, I know you can't teach GRIT to the GRITTIEST people on the face of the Earth. You can't teach GRIT to the descendants of Sojourner Truth, Fredrick Douglas, Crispus Attucks, W.E.B. Du Bois, Harriet Tubman, Booker T. Washington, Madam C. J. Walker, Nat Turner, Mary McLeod Bethune, and a plethora of others. You see, GRIT is a part of our DNA! It has been ingrained in us from the time we were ripped from our homeland. It became a part of us as we endured 400 years of slavery, it was woven into the fabric of our being during the Jim Crow era, through lynching, and the Civil Rights movement. GRIT is who we are; it is internally a part of us.

See, you can't teach GRIT, but what you can teach is to help kids learn from their failures. You can teach kids how to push forward after making a mistake. I learned a valuable concept during my time at the Outdoor Leadership Experience with the Missouri Leadership Academy. During this weekend opportunity, I learned the idea of "Failing Forward." Failing Forward is looking at how you push forward after failure, how do you make magic from a mistake. How do we, as educators, make it a priority to help students see the importance of learning from their mistakes while ensuring that every student is educated equitably, intentionally, and systematically and not by accident. We must help kids understand this final point, Failure is NOT an Option, but it is a part of the Process. So teach your students that their Failures should REFINE them, but they should NEVER DEFINE them. In doing this, you will cultivate and strengthen the GRIT that is already in their DNA!

Dr. VaShawn Smith (🐦@drvsmith) is the principal of Grandview Middle School in Grandview, Missouri. Dr. Smith earned his Doctorate of Educational Leadership from Saint Louis University in May of 2019. Prior to being named principal of Grandview Middle School, Dr. Smith served as an Assistant Principal, Instructional Coach, and Math teacher in Kansas, Ohio, and Nebraska. Dr. Smith has a Bachelor's Degree in Secondary Math Education, 2 Master's (Curriculum & Instruction, and Educational Administration and Supervision) all from the University of Nebraska, and Education Specialist Degree from Saint Louis University. Dr. Smith is the proud father of KaeShawn Smith, who will be starting her sophomore year at Xavier University in Louisiana this fall and is a Bio-Pre Med major. Dr. Smith is a member of Phi Beta Sigma Fraternity, Inc., and is currently the Missouri Director of Education for the Fraternity. Dr. Smith has also served as Director of Education for the Alpha Delta Sigma

Chapter in Kanas City, MO. Dr. Smith is the co-host of the AOS Podcast and co-founder of Black Males in Education of Greater Kansas City.

Overtly Fixed Racism In School Leadership

"My thought was that Malcolm would do good on your team because he is black." This assistant principal took whatever self-efficacy I had for this new school year in a new building and dismantled it in just a few words-- in a few seconds. She made this statement in a quick teacher huddle in the hallway right before my next class. I cannot remember quite exactly my response-- I just remember being numb and thinking to myself do not do anything that can cause me to lose my future in education. The end result-- I did nothing. I said nothing. I felt like I was nothing.

You see, prior to this moment, I was always a beloved teacher in every school community I touched. But here I was just a (N-word) who could reach other little (N-words). At that moment-- I tried to shrug it off and return to my teaching, but that moment was ingrained in my being for the duration of that year and, to some degree, still haunts me today. Am I an educator? That's the question that I asked myself each day. What does it mean to be an educator and to be black? I cannot go back to that moment and say the things that I should have said, but I can look at them right now and change the trajectory of so many flawed mindsets.

Since the conception of education in America-- education has been deemed as the great equalizer better known as the haves, and the have nots. Rather that was Pauper Schools in the early years in America to slaves risking death to read to now --education resources that are separated by zip codes that are right adjacent to each other. Are we blind? Why are there still educational laws or policies de facto or real that govern our mass education process? The fight for mass education was never about intellect -- but it was always liberty. The forefathers of America realized this before anyone even gave this any thought. And to that extent created the foundation for an impenetrable educational caste system. And in order to maintain the current caste system, people must think they are free while caged.

That year was my first year in a school, with the majority of the teachers being white with no more than five minority educators. I was outnumbered, ill-equipped, and to some degree, oblivious to the current state of minority educators. But I think about the Malcolms of our world. Or any marginalized student. I wonder--since that Assistant Principal saw me in that light, how does she see Malcolm? And that is how I was able to snap back to reality. How does she see Malcolm? How does she see Malcolm? This question resonates with me. It lingers within every fabric of my educational existence. How does she see Malcolm?

 I was raised by a God-Fearing woman who valued three things above all: God, Education, and an Oil Change / Tune-up. She would say that the third item was the only thing that Granddad could ever teach her about life--everything else came from Mama Cille. Most of my summers as a child were spent sitting at a desk that my mom borrowed-- from her classroom and I would do some type of work for at least 3-4 hours each day before I could do anything else. And after completion of the aforementioned schoolwork, then I would start on washing the woodworks-- that is the base of the walls inside the house among a list of other duties. What is most lasting about this memory is not the hate I gained for education because as a seven-year-old I had no idea why everyone else gets a summer break, but I do not-- but it was the perspective I gained. No matter what others say about me or think about me or misconstrue about me -- I know my self-worth-- it is defined in my work ethic that I was forced to create, as a seven-year-old. However, it laid dormant through many years of defiance from myself and trying hard not to be an A-student because I despised it. But now I see-- after 33 years-- I truly do see what my mother saw in me and what I see in every other little black boy. I see an untold story. A story that cannot be filled in by other people's prejudices. But a great story of life and discipline and love.

    Malcolms of the world may not be able to envision their full story yet-- but that is where I come in -- where we come in -- where black educators of the world come in with a desk during the summertime and a gallon full of pine sol water.

William Givens

(@williamthecore6) has been an educator for 13 years. His passion and self-motivation are rooted in a deep belief that every student and person can excel at something positive. He is currently an Advisor at the New Innovation School in Ferguson School District in St. Louis, Mo. William is also extremely involved in creating resources in St. Louis communities that have limited resources. His work with city officials and partnerships is the result of his powerful mission and values. William has dedicated his life to empowering communities with positive change through educational resourcefulness.

Protecting Black Bodies In St. Louis

Young Black men deal with many external and internal issues. These issues require constantly being on guard. In his book, *Between the World and Me*, Ta-Nehisi Coates (2015) describes this as protecting your body. As an adult Black man, like Coates and many others who look like us, young and old, this is what we have come to learn how to do; protect our bodies in an attempt to survive. Many times we do not have a choice of what neighborhoods we live in or the type of people we will encounter in those neighborhoods. Therefore, we had to remain in survival mode at all times. Coates describes, "To survive the neighborhoods and shield my body, I learned another language consisting of a basic complement of head nods and handshakes. I memorized a list of prohibited blocks" (23). I know that life all too well. Growing up in the inner-city streets of St. Louis, Missouri, I also knew what blocks and groups of people to avoid in my neighborhood too. It was a matter of safety and protecting my body.

Fortunately, when I was a child, school was my safe haven. It was a place I could go to escape the streets. I knew that during the eight hours of each day, five days per week, for ten months out of the year, I had somewhere I could be safe and not have to worry about protecting my body. I had teachers who cared about my peers and me. They genuinely seemed to want us to learn. Though I recall having very good experiences at school when I was young, I realize this is not true for all Black men, including some of my former students.

Protecting from the Dream Killers

Coates referred to The Dreamers, people who believe themselves to be white or have power over Black people (Coates, 2015). When I began my teaching career as an elementary school teacher, I taught in the City of St. Louis, Missouri. I accepted the charge of teaching a single-gender class of young, 3rd grade, Black and Brown males. Like Coates, and myself, these young men were growing up in an urban, inner-city neighborhood, in which from an early age, our access to a good education was not in the hands of anyone who looks like us, but mostly in the hands of The Dreamers.

The Dreamers of the school tried to warn me about the group of young men who I would be getting, but I refused to let their opinions cloud my judgment. As Coates points out, I also realized "fully 60 percent of all young black men who drop out of high school will go to jail" (27). I knew this was partly because some of The Dreamers around them had given up on them far too soon. I recognized I had to do something while I had these young men for ten months that would possibly keep them from being part of that statistic.

I recall a Dreamer who tried to have power over how I show up in the workplace as a Black male teacher. Adorned in my regular work attire of blazer, slacks, shirt, and tie, she said to me, "You dress up pretty nice for a teacher. You know it doesn't take all that." Representation matters. How I show up in these spaces matter; therefore, yes, it does take all that. Some Dreamers do not recognize or will not acknowledge the power of a Black man in the classroom. How are you showing up in these spaces?

Protecting Learning Spaces

In several places throughout his book, Coates talks about his school experiences in ways that are very unflattering. He states, "I came to see the streets and the schools as arms of the same beast" (33). Unlike myself, Coates did not see school as a getaway from the harsh realities of the neighborhood streets he had to maneuver to protect his body.

Over time, he came to see them as one and the same, places filled with failure, fear, and violence. "Fail in the streets, and the crews would catch you slipping and take your body. Fail in the schools, and you would be suspended and sent back to those same streets, where they would take your body" (33). When my students first came to me, some of them also had this same failure mentality. The Dreamers who they had for teachers in previous years helped to put them in this mind frame. Whenever they did something wrong, some of my students immediately requested to be sent to in-school suspension. Based on their previous learning experiences, if they did something wrong in the classroom, being pushed out of the learning environment was the punitive consequence. Coates felt his school was not revealing the truth to him, but concealing it instead. I imagine he was in a learning environment in which his thoughts, feelings, and curiosities lacked support. As a teacher, I worked to make sure my 3rd-grade students had an opposite learning experience. Not only did I teach them the academic skills I was required to do as part of my job, but I also incorporated character education into my everyday instruction. I did not have conversations with The Dreamers about my students, but instead avoided their negativity as much as possible and focused on my classroom. My students and I had real conversations about protecting their bodies. We talked about what some of The Dreamers of the world, some who taught in our very school, really thought of them and their ability to succeed. I taught them to be gentlemen. I taught them how to communicate and advocate for themselves; rather, it was in writing or verbally. I planted a seed. Are you planting seeds in your students? If you are not planting seeds, then water the seeds others have planted.

Protecting during Ferguson

Coates has a real conversation with his own son as he writes this book. It was a conversation about life experiences and having to protect his body from The Dreamers. He mentions his son's reaction as he stayed up late at night, on a school night, to hear if the verdict of the police officer who killed Michael Brown would result in an indictment. There was no indictment, and Coates recalls going into his young son's room after hearing him crying. He says, "I came in five minutes after, and I didn't hug you, and I didn't comfort you, because I thought it would be wrong to comfort you. I did not tell you that it would be okay because I have never believed it would be okay" (11). This was on Monday, November 24, 2014, around 8:24 p.m. This was in Ferguson, Missouri, which is a suburb of St. Louis, Missouri. This was happening right in our own city. All I could think about were my students. By this time, I had looped from 3rd grade to 5th grade with my single-gender classroom of Black and Brown male students. Similar to how Coates described his own son as he awaited the verdict my students "were young and still believed" (11). The district leaders made the decision to cancel school for the next day or two following the reading of the Michael Brown verdict, because they knew the rioting would start back up again, and they wanted students to be safe. It hurt that I was not able to see and talk to my students the next day to gauge their emotions. Unlike how Coates felt about comforting his son at this moment, I wanted to hug my students if they needed one, let them be curious and ask me questions, and for me to let them know it would be okay. I wanted them to know our city would eventually heal. However, until the healing began, in contrast to the teachers who Coates had when he was in school, I wanted my students to know they had a teacher who cared about protecting their body. Can you recall a time you wanted to protect your students' body, but could not? How did you feel?

Protecting in Unprecedented Times

In 2020, five years after the release of Coates' book, I am still trying to protect Black bodies in St. Louis, including my own. My former students are now in the 10th grade, and I am an elementary school principal. The COVID-19 pandemic has kept me away from my current students since March 13.

Their bodies need protection. Since then, Ahmaud Arbery, George Floyd, and many other black bodies are gone, and we are trying to get the world to agree that our lives matter. Once again, all I can do is think about my students because we are away from each other. Their bodies need protection. Who is protecting your body? Who is protecting your students' bodies?

As a school principal, I am trying to lead a school that is the opposite of the one Coates describes and unfortunately, had to experience in his neighborhood. I want my students to feel protected. I want them to explore their curiosity. I want them to know their teachers and administrators care about protecting their body and equipping them with knowledge. I want to provide them with a safe space where they can come and know failure is not an option, they have nothing to fear, and their body will have protection. Black male educators, wherever you are, we have a job to do: Protect Black Bodies!

Jim Triplett (@mredukator) has always been passionate about education and always strived for academic excellence. He graduated from high school in 1996 and matriculated to the University of Missouri-Columbia (Mizzou) on an academic scholarship. There, he became a member of Kappa Alpha Psi Fraternity, Inc. in 1998. He struggled academically at Mizzou and ultimately dropped out in 1999 to join the workforce.

Jim eventually became tired of just working retail jobs and was ready for a career. He felt a calling was on his life to educating others and began to work toward that goal. He re-enrolled in college and earned his Associate of Arts in

Teaching from St. Louis Community College in 2009 at the age of 30, 10 years after leaving Mizzou. In 2012, he obtained a Bachelor's degree in Early Childhood Education, with an emphasis on Urban Education, from Kennesaw State University (KSU) in Georgia. He graduated Magna Cum Laude and was the first African American male to graduate from the school's Urban Education Program. He joined Teach For America and was assigned to teach in the Saint Louis Public School District (SLPS).

In SLPS, Jim taught a single-gender classroom of 3rd-grade boys. He looped with them to 5th-grade, teaching academics and life/social skills such as being gentlemen, scholars, and leaders who have integrity. In 2014, in recognition of his work as a classroom teacher, he received the Pettus Award of Excellence from the SLPS Foundation and an Excellence in Education Award from the St. Louis American Foundation. In 2015, prior to leaving SLPS, Jim completed his Master's degree in Educational Technology through Lindenwood University. Jim went on to teach 3rd

Grade at a non-urban school in the Cobb County School District (Georgia). This experience clarified that an urban education environment was in better alignment with Jim's passion for being an educator.

In preparation for becoming a principal, in 2017, at the age of 38, Jim graduated from Harvard University's Graduate School of Education, receiving a Master of Education in School Leadership. Shortly after graduating from Harvard, Jim returned to SLPS and worked as an Academic Instructional Coach and an Assistant Principal. At the beginning of July 2019, 20 years after dropping out of Mizzou, he returned to Mizzou's campus as a Cohort 12 member of the College of Education's Doctor of Education in Educational Leadership and Policy Analysis program. While earning his fifth college degree, Jim is looking forward to finishing his deferred dream of graduating from Mizzou. He hopes his hard work, determination, and dedication is the motivation for his students, family, and friends to choose one of their deferred dreams; and realize it is never too late to pursue academic or personal goals.

Jim currently serves as principal of an elementary school in SLPS.

My Journey

I tend to be verbose, so I will apologize now. "I'm sorry." Now that's done, we are going on a circuitous journey on how I found my voice as an African American man, teacher, and leader. I have generalized and basic platitudes for life. I have some for understanding the importance of family and a few for my beliefs about education, my vocation. The purpose of our conversation is to help you understand how one man made his way through our educational system and our society.

My basic belief about life is pretty simplistic yet nebulous. I grew up as a member of a historic African American Baptist church. My sister and I were the fourth generation of my family to attend there. My mother was an aspiring professional singer. One of the songs she sang the most was If I Can Help Somebody. The song can be summed up in one line of its lyrics. If I can help somebody as I pass along, then my living shall not be in vain. My mother and maternal grandmother earnestly lived this message. My mother would never say "no" to anyone. She would run and run to help someone in need, to sing at a funeral or a church service, or to lend any of our, at times, limited resources. She did this while working four jobs to take care of two children as a single parent. There were times she only received rest when she passed out and ended up hospitalized. I noticed that my grandmother often helped people also. Many people in our family and in our church have lived with us over the years until they were able to get on their feet. Yet, she never passed out. She was never hospitalized. The reason why? She set boundaries. She told me once, "You can't help anybody if you dead. Then, they'll go right

along and ask the next person." I learned that balance is very important in life. There are very
few situations when extremism is positive.

My basic belief about family was taught to me by my same aforementioned grandmother,
who was all of four foot nine. Whenever a family member needed help, they called Momma Helen. My grandmother only had two children, yet over the years, many extended family members have lived in "Momma's" house. She was loving and forgiving yet very firm. She would often say, "I love you with all my heart, but when you are wrong, you wrong." She held everyone accountable. She was not afraid to challenge you: mentally, physically, or spiritually. I saw her do this day in and day out. She always put her family first, but she never upheld "wrongdoing". She was always willing to forgive you. She would even forget trespasses once you proved you were willing to change. What did I learn about family? Love your family, and forgive them when necessary. However, love is not acquiescence. You

show you care by challenging your family and loved ones to be better people.

    I have always loved going to school. From a very early age, there was never a time where I did not enjoy school. Wait. There was. The only time that I did not enjoy school was when I had to do schoolwork. However, every other time, I completely loved it! I was a social butterfly. I attended Euclid Montessori School from first grade through third. From there, I went to Classical Junior Academy, a magnet school. The discovery aspect of the Montessori educational process became my standard of interaction at school. I chose what and when I learned. Upon arriving at Classical, strangely, teachers would make "requests" of me and expect me to follow them! It was unnerving! Every day, every period, asking me to learn on "their," schedule! Classical was a magnet school for gifted students, so it didn't take me long to change my mindset and get with the program of a more traditional educational model. By my first year in college, I figured it out! I also damaged my GPA in the process. I tell all of my students my GPA in high school: 2.218. I loved learning, but I hated busy work. I realized my learning style and began to work efficiently. Eventually, I matured. But, most importantly, I failed. A lot. And really hard. I mean hard. Oh, and often. Very often. Through all this, I graduated. I still learned the material required of me. I was terrible at the processes of studying but excelled in acquiring information. Failure did not doom my future, nor will it doom any students'. In fact, it will strengthen them and help to give them direction.

There are a few men who I need to thank publicly for helping through my formative years. Thank you, Mr. Michael Collins. Thank you, Mr. Harold Grice. Thank you, Mr. Bert Bazemore. Thank you, Mr. Willie Royal. Thank you, Mr. Carl Hudson. These men are educators. These men influenced my life. All five men are African American. I was fortunate to have these men as part of my educational experience. From fourth grade through my senior year in high school, I have had at least two African American male teachers involved in my educational growth. Whenever I stepped out of line, they routinely stepped in for a conversation. While in high school, I attended a predominantly white school. Mr. Bazemore, Mr. Hudson, and occasionally Mr. Royal provided a safe space to vent, to talk, and to find me. I mentioned that I was not a great student and that I had poor study habits. Even so, I enjoyed challenging the thought processes of my teachers. Occasionally, I was put out of class or sent to the principal's office.

Whenever this happened, I knew I could talk to them or Mrs. Washington (the lone African American female teacher in the building) about the infraction. They told me the truth. They told me when something happened was unfair, when it was my fault or when it was probably both.

They taught me how to navigate in white spaces as an African American. More importantly, the men above taught me how to navigate white spaces as an African American male. African American male students walking through white spaces have to be hyper-aware of societal hazards. How often do white students matriculate through their educational journey without ever having a teacher that looked like them? Imagine being a white male student and never having a white male teacher. That would be unheard of to not have had a white male teacher – ever.

Imagine being a white female student, and you have never had a white female teacher – ever. When thinking through this rhetorical thought process, it seems absurd. Now imagine any white student never having a white teacher at any point in her or his educational career. Yet, when this happens with students of color, our society barely bats an eye. "It is normal." "Teaching is teaching, and a good teacher is a good teacher." "The race of a teacher is not really important if she or he is a competent teacher."

Teaching is so much more than simply instructing. A good teacher provides information and holds students accountable for learning. A great teacher builds authentic relationships with students, learns how they think, and encourages each child to be accountable for her or his own learning. The way in which the cultural history of our country has affected generations of black and brown bodies call for the need for great teachers. The educational system was not created to benefit people who look like me. Who think like me? Many "good" teachers, whether purposeful or not, attempted to stifle my thinking and my growth. "Great" teachers taught me to understand myself, to understand my culture, and how to navigate society. The five men were, no, *are* great teachers. They are excellent examples for me. They held me accountable. We had conversations outside of the classroom that benefited me on my journey. When I teach, that is my goal for every child, but especially for every little brown boy that looks like me. My job as a teacher is not only to teach them the curriculum but to help them learn how to navigate life in a society that views you as unworthy.

So what did I learn? I learned that we should challenge the people we care about to make them stronger. I challenge you. You challenge me. If you are unwilling to call me out when I am wrong, that means that you do not care about me, and I should not trust you nor your motives. I learned that all people, especially students, should be allowed to learn from their mistakes. Challenge each student. Tell them when they are wrong. Then be there for them as they figure out how to fix their own mistakes. This teaches metacognition and reflection. It teaches them how, empathetically, to help others through their mistakes. More importantly, it teaches them when to allow people to struggle, so that they become better.

In summation, I learned the importance of challenging those we care about and allowing them to make mistakes, take accountability, and then to grow stronger. They gain the ability to find her or his own balance. They will be able to reflect and to decide what is essential and what is not. They will have the skillset and intrinsic desire to balance their own lives and still be able to benefit society as a whole. The men above helped me to find my own balance, but more significantly, they showed me that I need to attempt to be a "great" teacher to all students.

Especially the brown boys that look like me. My job is to lift them up so they can lift the next generation.

Neil Daniels, II (@mastermind4club) was born in St. Louis, MO, and is a product of the St. Louis Public School Magnet program. He also took part in the desegregation program during high school. After high school, he went on to attend Fontbonne College (now, Fontbonne University) and graduated with a degree in Public Relations. He worked in communications and competitor analysis at BJC Health System. Then, a transition was made to work in and, eventually, to help lead the Outreach and Education Department at Care Partners MC+ Medicaid HMO. Life changes and the selling off of Care Partners to AmeriHealth Mercy, who disbanded the company, led to spending time at home as a stay at home dad. After a little more than a year, he began to rebuild his career. He sold insurance part-time and worked at a national healthcare HMO. During this time, he noticed a pattern and found his passion. At each job, he learned how to listen to people who were often frustrated and found joy in educating people and helping them to problem-solve. So, he quit his job to become a paraprofessional in Special School District and to obtain a master's degree in education.

Neil learned to listen to children to help them learn and grow. Many of the students that he worked with brought trauma with them to school. He learned how to put children's needs first and still to encourage them to learn. Once becoming a teacher, he became a leader within his school and district by applying the same skills with adults. He is the treasurer of his local union and has been part of three district negations in nine years. He has been a staunch advocate for ALL students and teachers. He has been a Diversity in Action leader at the school and district level. He has worked to create programs for new teachers with Missouri National Education Association. He, also, has led school and district level professional development around social justice and understanding varying perspectives. He is currently in the process of completing his doctoral work in educational administration.

Mentor Armor

"What you see and what you hear depends a great deal on where you are standing. It also depends on what sort of person you are."

— **C.S. Lewis**

Personal experiences influence our perception of ourselves and our surroundings. We engage things that confirm or disprove our beliefs. This cognitive function is imperative for personal growth and development. In a healthy environment, positive role models are ample, wisdom gleaned from experiences is shared freely, and identities and natural talents are affirmed. Every element of a healthy culture impacts the mental perception of a child. He or she studies what is taught, imitates what is seen, and ponders what is heard. The influences of an unhealthy environment are just as impactful. An individual's mental perception is engrafted within social constructs that are reflective in one's physical, mental, and emotional health.

Though some individuals are intrinsically inspired to challenge social norms that are detrimental to their wellbeing, many do not. Without tools of self-reflecting, questioning external stimuli, or challenging negative norms, individual perception is limited. Metacognition abated may result in a lack of resolution of conflict, lowered efficacy, and poor self-perception. Negative environmental and media influences compounded with malignant neglect have decimated the mental perception of numerous children in underserved communities. The outcome has left factions of our parental and political community baffled with no sustainable resolution in sight. Ironically, unsuccessful attempts to incentivize children have left interventionists with negative perceptions of the very communities they tried to aid.

Mental Armor is a school-friendly program that presents a resolution for children who have adapted to negative social constructs. A mindful approach is implemented to support children in self-reflecting, questioning external stimuli, and challenging negative norms. By aiding the positive development of mental perceptions, students are empowered to reason resolution, increase self-efficacy, and have positive self-perception. Students will also identify and question the mental perception of peers and the impact of environmental and media influences. Each child will have a systemic impact on their family, peers, and community.

Bryan Smith (🐦@cultivatinge) grew up in a small town in western Kentucky with his siblings in a close Christian community. Living in a single-parent household, Bryan experienced economic, social, and cultural hardships. "I never really paid attention to the fact that my father was missing. We never had time to feel the void," stated Bryan Smith. New challenges occurred once his family relocated to a city in Georgia. "When we moved, poverty became the backdrop of our lives. Alcoholism, drugs, gangs, and the threat of "lack" competed daily with our family values, faith, and resiliency," Bryan recalled. Eventually returning to Kentucky, Bryan pursued his degree in Education and School Guidance Counseling. He now uses his past experiences to inspire others.

Outro

The spirit within each of us contains a singular history, layered in stories that speak to the hills and valleys of our lives. Our life is not merely shaped by our own doing, but conducted by a maestro in front of a 400 piece orchestra. The maestro's wand moves through the air with strength and conviction, slicing the void with great ease. Here we must make it clear of the arena we are in. This symphony is composed of the pieces of our consciousness that are working overtime each and every hour of the day—contemplating self-worth. Problem-solving health and safety. Strategizing the means to contribute, remain reserved, and protect the very essence of what makes us whole.

What makes us unique? Our authenticity. The maestro looks across the ensemble looking at all of the pieces. All of the sets of eyes stare, looking at an imposter with the wand and staring with apprehension and caution for the unknown, in the maestro's untold motives. Each set of eyes represents pride, hope, ambitions, faith, authority, creed, insecurities, and fear of not fulfilling their potential or calling. The eyes blink in unison to keep the conductor in focus. Not to keep the rhythm or maintain the syncopation of the notes but to not be surprised or caught off guard. To not be caught by the intentions of hate, racism, and systemic control of the lives and soul of the musicians. The maestro again looks over the orchestra and stares deep into those eyes, searching for despair and distress.

At the first strike of the tempo change, the maestro did not find anguish in the seats of the musicians, because they are unified. Tied together by the complex commonality of lived experiences. These experiences, when moving together, become a rallying cry for the authentic sound within each Black Male Educator. This rumbling tone comes from the musicians, orchestrating a beautiful symphony of voices. Whether your personal story is marred in pain or cast aside. Your experiences are who you are...and your voice commands to be heard like a roaring melody.

The stage has always been yours to command with great authority. As my cofounder alluded to, command the narrative and direct your path. This *Voices* publication encapsulated stories from across our region, and they live within each of us. Tell your story. Be authentic. Use your Voice.

-**Dr. Darryl Diggs Jr.** (@achievement4all)

Voices by BMESTL
Vol. 2 Archiving 2020
JANUARY 2021
Submit your essay now at bmestl.com/voices2

Made in the USA
Monee, IL
17 August 2020